A Helping Hand

A REFLECTION GUIDE
FOR THE DIVORCED,
WIDOWED OR SEPARATED

James L. Horstman
Van T. Moon

Paulist Press   *New York/Mahwah*

Book Design by Nighthawk Design.

Library of Congress Cataloging-in-Publication Data

Horstman, James L., 1945–
   A helping hand / James L. Horstman, Van T. Moon.
     p. cm.
   ISBN 0-8091-3400-4
   1. Divorce—Religious aspects—Christianity—Meditations.
   2. Bereavement—Religious aspects—Christianity—Meditations.
   3. Divorced people—Prayer-books and devotions—English.
   4. Widowers—Prayer-books and devotions—English. 5. Widows—
Prayer-books and devotions—English. 6. Spiritual journals—
Authorship. I. Moon, Van T., 1926– . II. Title.
   BV4596.D58H67   1993
   248.8'6—dc20   93-15070
                                                  CIP

Published by Paulist Press
997 Macarthur Boulevard
Mahwah, New Jersey 07430

Printed and bound in the
United States of America

Contents ────────────────────

Introduction   vii

Journaling: A Must   ix
    How to Journal Properly   x
    How to Use This Book   xii

ICEBREAKERS

Getting to Know Myself   3
Looking at Myself   5

GRIEF

Hurt   9
Five Stages of Grief   11
Dealing with Grief   16
Alone or Lonely?   18
Reconciliation   20

SELF-ESTEEM

How Do You Feel About Responsibility?   25
How Do You See Yourself—A Winner or a Loser?   27
How Do Others See You?   29

Regret	31
The Sweat Shirt Game	33
Self-Esteem	35
Self-Growth	37
Resentment	39

SPIRITUAL GROWTH

God's Love	43
Disappointment	45
Christian Living	47
Love	49
Talking to God	51

FORGIVENESS

Forgiveness	55
Love Your Enemies	57
"I Wish I Had Said . . ."	59
Do You Enjoy Hating?	61
How Can I Learn To Forgive?	63

SEXUALITY

Sexual Attitudes	67
Single Again—What Is My Attitude About Sex?	69
Sexual Conduct	71

TRUST

Trusting 75
Being Single 77
Seeking Support 79
Trust in Self 81
Stages of Trust 83
Feelings 85
Sometimes I Need a Friend 87

PARENTING

Parenting 91
Single Parenting 93
Thoughts on Single Parenting 95
Single Parenting Problems 97

SPECIAL PROBLEMS

How Would You Handle This? 101
Where Do I Fit In? 103
With Friends Like This . . . 105
Tomorrow 107

VALUES

Lost in a Lifeboat 111
Complete the Thought 113
The Nuclear War 115

Abigail   117
Perception Triads   119

FUN IN GENERAL

Minimum Level   123
Think So?   125

Introduction _____

*W*elcome to the world of healing. Let us take the liberty of saying that the mere fact that you have opened this little book is evidence enough that you recognize you have a need to go on to a new life and you are searching for some answers.

That having been established, permit us to go on and say that we love you even though we do not know you and you do not know us. You are probably saying to yourself, "How can you say that? It doesn't make sense."

We are not saying that we are "in love" with you, only that we love you in the same way that God asked us to love one another, be with one another, respect one another, help one another, and not to judge or condemn one another.

The maze of strong feelings that you have felt and are still experiencing are only natural. "No they are not," you say. "No one feels like this; no one knows the hurts and frustration that I am feeling." Well you are partially right. You are right in that none of us can know the depths of these feelings unless we have been through it also. Then these feelings are quite familiar.

We, the authors, are not strangers to these feelings since both of us have been through what you are experiencing. And we do mean all of them, from the deepest depression and hate on through anger, grief, frustration, resentment, and on and on. Yes, all of them.

The loss of a spouse ranks 1, 2, and 3 on the rating scale of *"Social Readjustment Ratings."* Death of a spouse, divorce, and separation from a spouse are the first three greatest stress situations you can experience. So we can say that we do know of your hurt, anger, and frustration first-hand, and we know of the effects on one's life.

But we can also say that because God wants all of us to "have life and enjoy it to the fullest," he has in his compassion and love for us provided us with healing, and that process of healing is available to you. This we can also say from experience, because we too have been through the process.

We welcome you to this healing process. It is one of discovery and recovery. What you have experienced and are still going through is tough business, but you will be healed. Be confident in knowing that not only do you want to be healed, but we want it, and, most importantly, God wants it for you. And now with your participation, help is here. It starts with this book.

Journaling—A Must _____

To some people, journaling will be somewhat foreign or strange, and to some it will be a challenge, and yet to some others who have journaled in the past it will seem like second nature. It is to the first two groups that we would like to make these comments. Journaling, we have discovered, is a very therapeutic exercise. We cannot underline enough the merit of journaling at this time in your life when reading this book. We realize that to some it will be somewhat laborious until you get into the routine of it. But believe us when we say that it is most necessary and, as you will discover, rewarding and effective to your healing process.

One of the many difficult adjustments we make after the death of a marriage or a spouse is to transfer our focus and attention away from reaction to our former spouse and onto ourselves. Is this selfish? Not at all, because now you have to get to know yourself better than ever before. "Who am I now? How am I emotionally, mentally, spiritually, even physically? What is being said to me about myself in this painful time of adjustment? How about my lifestyle, or just style? . . . unresolved personal issues? . . . past or recent wounds?" These and many other personal reflection questions can lead you to a deeper awareness of who you are, and put you in touch with a new depth of knowledge that maybe you were not aware existed within you. Journaling also helps you to develop new levels of seeking knowledge of ourselves and new skills for intimacy with ourselves and God, notwithstanding once these new levels are attained and these new skills are sharpened and loved, they prepare you for a new life of understanding others and thus leading to a better awareness in new relationships that may come.

Journal writing is a proven and concrete way we acknowledge ourselves as someone with whom we can dialogue comfortably. When we value the commitment to journal, we are making a commitment to expressing and hearing ourselves out. We are saying there is a presence, a precious person within us that deserves to be known if we are to become integrated in our minds, heart and wisdom. Unfortunately some of us seem to hear: "There is no one in there, no one at home inside." To those who sense that feeling, dismiss it with haste because there is someone home, some very special person whom God created and loved infinitely and is waiting to be discovered by no one else but you. Journaling then becomes a very beautiful and rewarding experience of discovering the self that may have been lost or at best subdued for years, even before a divorce or death experience. So we invite you to use these reflection questions presented in this book of journey into your truest self which is the meeting place with God.

HOW TO JOURNAL PROPERLY

Journaling Book: Purchase some type of notebook—a spiral one, or a three-ring notebook (more flexible and expandable), or a diary. Most bookstores handle a variety of such notebooks. Take the attitude that this is going to be a very valuable book to you in the future.

Journaling Place: Most people who journal find it advisable and helpful to have a regular journaling place—a place safe for you, a place even sacred to you to be with yourself, a place where you can most likely be alone and free from interruption, a place uncluttered and comfortable, a place where you can feel a sense of separateness. All of these will add to the validity and completeness of your journey inward.

What To Write: There is no right way to journal. There are some methods that may be helpful for exploring your responses to a question:

(a) Write whatever comes to you after reading the question. Be spontaneous on the thoughts, feelings, reactions that come up. Do not analyze or figure out what the question is trying to expose. The answer is to expose the real you to you.

(b) Read over what you have written and underline the feelings you have expressed. If you don't see feelings described in your writing, ask yourself what are the feelings connected to your thoughts and experiences and write them in, somewhere around the thought they provoked. Identifying feelings is an important part of the healing process. Be honest, because the true you is waiting to be revealed. Some feelings will surprise you, some might mystify you or shock you, but they will help you to see you as you are, and that is the real revelation you are seeking.

(c) Ask yourself how you now feel about what you wrote. For example, "I'm surprised to read I felt relief," or "I didn't realize I was so angry," or "Why did the feeling hide itself so completely or for so long?" This way you will call out true feelings both past and present, and you can see into the truth of it and recognize yourself as you are. Important note of caution: Be careful not to judge what you have written. This is not a test to pass nor is it for the public to see. It should be the whole truth without any punishment or prize, unless of course the prize is self-knowledge. Sometimes confusion or painful expressions that come out on paper are an important mirror of what is going on inside. Maybe more than a mirror may be a self-portrait that you are painting. You may even recognize a flaw that you can correct with a slight touch of the master's brush so that when you are finished you will have accomplished the most accurate reproduction of the real, new you that God created. Once these thoughts and feelings are outside ourselves we can recognize them, deal with them and the healing process can continue.

(d) Write your hopes and wishes on each topic or question. This is an important way to get in touch with unexpected possibilities or needs, and it helps you to dream for the future and what we ultimately really need—a desire for the growth to a better you, one who is more acceptable to you and to God.

(e) Don't hurry. Take your time. Don't let it become a chore. Let it become an experience of seeking something you really want and desire. Look forward to journaling; let it become your best friend. Learn to trust it, confide in it, value it, and you will discover that the real value is a better you.

(f) Lastly, we are including a list of feeling words. Read them and bring them up to a conscious level so that they are readily usable to you. Don't stereotype them. Look for the ones that really express your true feelings. Good luck and God be with you.

HOW TO USE THIS BOOK

In order to get the most out of the use of this book, we would like to make some suggestions on how you can use this book most effectively.

When using it on your own (without the support group manual): Study the section on journaling carefully. Ask questions (if need be) of those who have had experience journaling, or refer to the section on journaling.

Determine the area of healing you need right now.

These exercises are *not* in any special order. The proper order is based solely on your current and most urgent need. For example, you may feel that your personal need right now is in Trust. If so, choose a topic from that section first. You may wish to move around the topics within the section before you select another section. Or you may want to take one exercise from each topic within the section you selected to start with. From there you may want to select Forgiveness or Grief or some other section. But make your priority in the selection of the section first and then a topic within that section.

At the end of each topic there are several questions that are to be answered in your journal. Take only *one* at a time. Do not try to go through all the questions at a single sitting. First read the scripture slowly and understand what God's message is saying. Read it several times if necessary. Then read the PRAYER/MEDITATION slowly. At the end, stop and think about what you have read; then select *one* question and begin to journal on that question. Write all you can about that one question and then stop. At the next sitting reread the readings and the prayer and then select a second question and write on that question.

This accomplishes two things: first, it makes you slow down and get in touch with yourself, and, second, it calls you to a more complete process for your personal growth. Remember, you are not in a hurry and you are not reading a novel.

Repeat each step for each question, and when you have completed all the questions, review what you have written. Now summarize your conclusions from all your writings. Then select another topic—it may be in the same section or in a completely different section—and repeat the above steps. Be sure to save all that you have written in your journal. In three to six months go back and review what you have written on each topic in each section. You will be amazed to discover how far you have come on your journey of healing.

For those of you who are members of a support group that use the "HELPING HANDS" manual: Sections and topics for your group will probably be determined by the program chairman. The program chairman is trying to select a program that will serve the needs of most of the group.

A HELPING HAND, unlike the "Helping Hands" manual, is to be used on your own for your own personal growth. You may want to follow the same programs that have been selected by your group, or because of the issues you are dealing with at this time, you may wish to select a section and topic that is more vital to you needs. If you are choosing to deal with a different section than your group, let your thoughts about your needs be known to the program chairman or support group leader. Remember that there may be other people in your group who are in the same place as you.

Follow the steps about journaling as they apply. Make abundant use of the feeling word list. These words may help you express your feelings better and understand yourself more completely.

Icebreakers

Getting To Know Myself

Acts 11:1–10

All through Judea the apostles and the brothers heard that
Gentiles, too, had accepted the word of God. As a result, when
Peter went up to Jerusalem some among the circumcised took
issue with him, saying, "You entered the house of uncircum-
cised men and ate with them." Peter then explained the whole
affair to them step by step from the beginning: "I was at prayer
in the city of Joppa when, in a trance, I saw a vision. An object
like a big canvas came down; it was lowered down to me from
the sky by its four corners. As I stared at it I could make out
four-legged creatures of the earth, wild beasts and reptiles, and
birds of the sky. I listened as a voice said to me, 'Get up, Peter!
Slaughter, then eat.' I replied: 'Not for a moment, sir! Nothing
unclean or impure has ever entered my mouth!'" A second time
the voice from the heavens spoke out: 'What God has purified
you are not to call unclean.' This happened three times; then
the canvas with everything in it was drawn up again into the sky.

PRAYER/MEDITATION

O Lord, thank you for caring for me and thank you for helping
me to see myself in a new light. Thank you for the gift of new
friends and their understanding and acceptance. I now can see
and recognize my feeling of rejection and being considered

unclean. Lord, let your love shine upon me and bring me out of my darkness and into your light, enabling me to see that through you all good things shall come. Amen.

Reflections

What do I know about myself and my personality?

What evils do I now face as a challenge for me to slaughter?

What qualities do I have and which ones do I prefer to find in friends?

What kind of values do I now ascribe to those qualities?

Looking at Myself

Acts 9:36–41

Now in Joppa there was a certain woman convert named Tabitha. Her life was marked by constant good deeds and acts of charity. At about that time she fell ill and died. They washed her body and laid it out in an upstairs room. Since Lydda was near Joppa, the disciples who had heard that Peter was there sent two men to him with the urgent request, "Please come over to us without delay." Peter set out with them as they asked. Upon his arrival they took him upstairs to the room. All the widows came to him in tears and showed him the various garments Tabitha had made when she was still with them. Peter first made everyone go outside; then he knelt down and prayed. Turning to the dead body, he said, "Tabitha, stand up." She opened her eyes, then looked at Peter and sat up. He gave her his hand and helped her to her feet. The next thing he did was to call in those who were believers and the widows to show them that she was alive.

PRAYER/MEDITATION

Jesus, I feel very humbled by the stories I have recently heard and finding loving people who will listen to me and my story with compassion. Guide me on to my recovery and give me strength to continue this painful journey. Help me deal with the hurt that I feel inside. And help me to get past the pain, so that I may understand the suffering I have gone through and count the blessings in my life. I take courage in your words to "stand up" knowing that you are with me. This I pray through Christ our Lord. Amen.

Reflections

Is the experience of stepping out and joining a group as painful as you thought it would be?

Have you witnessed people who are healing or who have been healed?

How do you feel now in comparison to the fear you felt before?

Can you accept God's challenge to "stand up" and to live again?

Grief

Hurt

Luke 23:32-43

Two others who were criminals were led along with him to be crucified. When they came to Skull Place, as it was called, they crucified him there and the criminals as well, one on his right and the other on his left. They divided his garments, rolling dice for them. The people stood there watching, and the leaders kept jeering at him, saying, "He saved others; let him save himself if he is the Messiah of God, the chosen one." The soldiers also made fun of him, coming forward to offer him their sour wine and saying, "If you are the king of the Jews, save yourself." There was an inscription over his head: "THIS IS THE KING OF THE JEWS." One of the criminals hanging in crucifixion blasphemed him: "Aren't you the Messiah? Then save yourself and us." But the other one rebuked him: "Have you no fear of God, seeing you are under the same sentence? We deserve it, after all. We are only paying the price for what we've done, but this man has done nothing wrong." He then said, "Jesus, remember me when you enter upon your reign." And Jesus replied, "I assure you: this day you will be with me in paradise."

PRAYER/MEDITATION

Dear Jesus, I never realized before the hurt you must have felt hanging on the cross, abandoned by friends, rejected by acquaintances and rebuked by strangers. Now these feelings are so strong in me that I call on you who know how I feel—abandoned, alone, and lonely. Give me the strength you showed in forgiving all of us our sins. I really need your help. I cry out to you in my despair to show me your love so that I can learn to love again and fulfill your commandment to love one another. For this I pray. Amen.

Reflections

Think about how God helped you through your pain. Does that help you to understand in a deeper dimension?

Deepen your faith and believe the words of Jesus, "Ask and it will be given, seek and you will find." Express your feelings and thoughts.

In remembering the "hurts" that you have had, how have you worked through them?

What growth have you experienced from the hurts and how have you felt after the healing process?

Five Stages of Grief

1 Corinthians 15:35–44

Perhaps someone will say, "How are the dead to be raised up? What kind of body will they have?" A nonsensical question! The seed you sow does not germinate unless it dies. When you sow, you do not sow the full-blown plant, but a kernel of wheat or some other grain. God gives body to it as he pleases, and to each seed its own fruition. Not all bodily nature is the same. Men have one kind of body, animals another. Birds are of their kind, fish are of theirs. There are heavenly bodies and there are earthly bodies. The splendor of the heavenly bodies is one thing, that of the earthly another. The sun has a splendor of its own, so has the moon, land and the stars have theirs. Even among the stars, one differs from another in brightness. So is it with the resurrection of the dead. What is sown in the earth is subject to decay, what rises is incorruptible, What is sown is ignoble, what rises is glorious. Weakness is sown, strength rises up. A natural body is put down and a spiritual body comes up.

PRAYER/MEDITATION

Heavenly Father, dealing with my grief seems like such a mountain before me. I have faith in your words, "The seed you sow does not germinate until it dies." Help me, Lord, to let my grief die so that I may grow into a new being to become what you have planned for me. It seems insurmountable for me alone, but with your help all things are obtainable. Let me see my past life as already sown and in decay, so that I can grow in the experience of what it is to come into your glory. Through Christ our Lord. Amen.

The five stages of grief are: denial, bargaining, anger, depression, and acceptance.

GRIEF

When we lose someone we love, we go through a process we refer to as grief. Grief has several distinctive stages and we go through all of them in time. Some pass quicker than others and they do not have to be in any particular order. Some may even come back or reoccur more than once. So the order in which they are listed may not be the way they occur for you. Also at any time throughout the grief process, you may experience physical problems, like weight loss, nervousness, insomnia, or body aches or pains. If they persist, see your doctor.

DENIAL

When you are in denial, you find it hard to accept the loss. It may be especially hard if it occurred suddenly. You are reluctant to admit that the marriage is over. "This is not happening to me." An emotional shock may set in and last for days. Denial is normal; it acts as a buffer for or against something too overwhelming to accept at the time. It gives you time to regroup yourself to face reality. The denial stage is a period of fantasy, but the danger is to accept the fantasy as reality. Gradually one moves from fantasy and denial to reality and goes into another stage.

ANGER

You will feel angry, or want to blame, whatever or whoever you see as the cause of the loss. You may even get angry or blame yourself. Many people get angry at God for allowing it to happen and not preventing the loss. Or you may get angry at the person you lost for leaving you behind, an angry feeling of abandonment. Your anger may also stem from a feeling of helplessness that you cannot do anything to change the situation. All this anger needs to be appropriately expressed and acknowledged, but all too often it is expressed physically or openly. Tears may camouflage the anger, or the anger may be hidden or internalized in physical ailments, like stomach problems or headaches.

BARGAINING

In bargaining we set up conditions, both real and imaginary, so that we do not have to face the reality of what has happened to us. We may bargain with God to "fix" the situation. If you are divorced, you may bargain with your ex-spouse. Or you may say, to yourself or others, that "if only" things were back to normal you would change or do something different.

DEPRESSION

Depression can be the most difficult feeling to overcome. You use a lot of energy to suppress the anger and hurt, and there is very little energy left over for day to day activities. You seem to have no energy left, you have trouble concentrating, you withdraw from people, and you become unable to perform even routine activities. Do not let yourself get too discouraged, for you will eventually move out of this stage.

ACCEPTANCE

Eventually you will come to a point when you will begin to accept the loss and the reality of the situation. You can remember without the pain. You start to look forward to living again, you have hope for your future, and you begin to rebuild your life. You accept the loss and the pain will heal.

Do not ignore your feelings. Talk when you feel like talking and cry when you feel like crying. Remember, no matter how difficult life may seem, you will get through the grieving process. It just takes some time, and the time it takes will vary from person to person. But the more you do for yourself, the shorter the time will be.

Reflections

When you examine the five stages of grief, do you recognize the ones you still have to deal with? Where are you now?

Take some positive action on those you are dealing with and set some goals to deal with them.

How can you allow the old seeds to decay so that new life may bloom?

Can you recognize your own weakness and helplessness to control life and begin to let go and let God choose a new life for you?

Dealing with Grief

Psalm 6

O Lord, reprove me not in your anger, nor chastise me in your wrath. Have pity on me, O Lord, for I am languishing; heal me, O Lord, for my body is in terror; My soul, too, is utterly terrified; but you, O Lord, how long . . . ? Return, O Lord, save my life; rescue me because of your kindness, for among the dead no one remembers you; in the nether world who gives you thanks? I am wearied with sighing; every night I flood my bed with weeping; I drench my couch with my tears. My eyes are dimmed with sorrow; they have aged because of all my foes. Depart from me, all evildoers, for the Lord has heard the sound of my weeping. The Lord has heard my plea; the Lord has accepted my prayer. All my enemies shall be put to shame in utter terror; they shall fall back in sudden shame.

PRAYER/MEDITATION

Dear Lord, in you I take refuge. Relieve me of the grief in my life. Save me from my depression and rescue me. Grief is my enemy, and I call on you for help to bind the evil one from continuing this war against me. Arm me with your love and allow me to do battle with my pain. Arm me with your sword of forgiveness and the helmet of your compassion to defeat the loneliness I feel inside. And let me raise up your shield before me so that I may understand the suffering I have gone through, deal with the hurt I feel inside, and count the blessings in my life. Amen.

Reflections

What can you do to sustain patience during your battle for recovery? Life changes while you are dealing with grief, and not all for the good. How can you deal more effectively with the problems? You know you cannot control the events that caused you grief, but you can, through healing, accept the past, and come to a new understanding. What are some ways to accept the past? With God's help, you can control your feelings, your life, and your future. But can you be happy?

Alone or Lonely?

Psalm 23

The Lord is my shepherd; I shall not want. In verdant pastures he gives me repose; Beside restful waters he leads me; he refreshes my soul. He guides me in right paths for his name's sake. Even though I walk in the dark valley I fear no evil; for you are at my side with your rod and your staff that give me courage.

You spread the table before me in the sight of my foes; you anoint my head with oil; my cup overflows. Only goodness and kindness follow me all the days of my life; and I shall dwell in the house of the Lord for years to come.

PRAYER/MEDITATION

Lord, help me when I am feeling lonely. I know you have said you are always with me and I am never alone, but it is hard for me not to feel lonely. I have never felt so alone before, and I feel so destroyed, hopeless and abandoned. Help me to recognize that you are there for me. Guide me to the realization that alone is not the same as lonely. I have heard people say: "keep busy," "do things," "join groups," but I still come home alone and feel the emptiness around me. Let me be aware of your presence always so that I may overcome the way I feel. I ask this through Christ our Lord. Amen.

Reflections

Write out how you feel about being alone and lonely. What are some of the benefits of being alone, and how can you make the most of that time?

Being alone can have great benefits, and being lonely can be conquered by new friends and activities. How can you deal with these two separately?

Read Isaiah 49:15–16.

Think of something you always wanted to do, but because your spouse did not share your desires, you did not. Now you can—so go for it!

Reconciliation

John 4:19–24

"Sir," answered the woman, "I can see you are a prophet. Our ancestors worshiped on this mountain, but you people claim that Jerusalem is the place where men ought to worship God." Jesus told her: "Believe me, woman, an hour is coming when you will worship the Father neither on this mountain nor in Jerusalem. You people worship what you do not understand, while we understand what we worship; after all, salvation is from the Jews. Yet an hour is coming, and is already here, when authentic worshipers will worship the Father in Spirit and truth. Indeed, it is just such worshipers the Father seeks. God is Spirit, and those who worship him must worship in Spirit and truth."

PRAYER/MEDITATION

Lord, I realize that the story of the woman at the well is a story about reconciliation. You have given us the eternal promise that if we know you and do your will, you will give us life-giving water, never to thirst again. But I find it so hard to forgive and reconcile the hate, resentfulness, and anger that I feel inside. Lord, let me find the strength and ability to overcome the evil within, so that I may taste the living water and rediscover my inner peace. For this I pray. Amen.

Reflections

How can I learn from Christ to overcome the feelings of hate, resentfulness, and anger?

When I see these feelings in others, how does it make me feel?

How can I heal my self-esteem, so that the rest of my life can be happy and fulfilled? Write out specific objectives.

Since I have been given free will, what must I do now?

Self-Esteem

How Do You Feel About Responsibility?

Psalm 139:1–12

O Lord, you have probed me and you know me; you know when I sit and when I stand; you understand my thoughts from afar. My journeys and my rest you scrutinize, with all my ways you are familiar. Even before a word is on my tongue, behold, O Lord, you know the whole of it. Behind me and before, you hem me in and rest your hand upon me. Such knowledge is too wonderful for me, too lofty for me to attain. Where can I go from your spirit? From your presence where can I flee? If I go up to the heavens, you are there; if I sink to the nether world, you are present there. If I take the wings of the dawn, if I settle at the farthest limits of the sea, even there your hand shall guide me, and your right hand hold me fast. If I say, "Surely the darkness shall hide me, and night shall be my light"—for you darkness itself is not dark, and night shines as the day.

PRAYER/MEDITATION

Father in heaven, I recognize that I am unique. Unique in body, soul, intellect and a free will. But it is my free will, Lord, that sometimes causes me to stumble. I make decisions that do not turn out the way I had planned, and I deny any wrongdoings. I wonder why you gave us a free will. I would like to blame others for my faults or the plans that I have made that did not turn out as I had thought. But you also have given us the gift of intelligence, so I can learn, accept, and know from my past. And now I must recognize that I, and no one else, am responsible for what I do, say, and feel. So give me the strength and guide me, Lord, through the hours and days of my life. For this I pray. Amen.

Reflections

Am I responsible for everything in my life?

Am I responsible for what others think?

The tendency to blame others for the bad things that happen to me is so easy. Are they ever responsible? How can I guard myself from this tendency?

In what other ways am I unique? (Romans 12:6–8)

Read Lamentations 3:22–24.

How Do You See Yourself—
A Winner or a Loser?

John 14:1–4

Do not let your hearts be troubled. Have faith in God and faith in me. In my Father's house there are many dwelling places; otherwise, how could I have told you that I was going to prepare a place for you? I am indeed going to prepare a place for you, and then I shall come back to take you with me, that where I am you also may be. You know the way that leads where I go.

PRAYER/MEDITATION

Heavenly Father, I come to you in confusion and despair. The hurts I have experienced have left deep wounds in me that will not heal. I feel less of a person than I used to; I feel that I am no longer loved or respected. My self-esteem is low and yet I hear the promises of your grace, your love, and your compassion for me. But it is hard to accept them in my present state of mind. So I cry out to you. Heal my hurts. Restore in me my faith in myself and strengthen in me my faith in you. Help me see that your love for me has not vanished, and give me back my confidence. For I know that with you by my side I am a winner. Amen.

Reflections

How have the loser character traits affected my living and my life style?

What must I do to overcome those negative character traits?

"God did not send the Son into the world to condemn the world, but that the world might be saved through him" (John 3:17). How can I stop judging myself and serve our Lord Jesus Christ?

"A lamp to my feet is your word, a light to my path" (Psalm 119:105). How do you interpret this? How do you implement this in your own life?

How Do Others See You?

Psalm 31:1–6

In you, O Lord, I take refuge; let me never be put to shame. In your justice rescue me, incline your ear to me, make haste to deliver me! Be my rock of refuge, a stronghold to give me safety. You are my rock and my fortress; for your name's sake you will lead and guide me. You will free me from the snare they set for me, for you are my refuge. Into your hands I commend my spirit; you will redeem me, O Lord, O faithful God.

PRAYER/MEDITATION

Loving God, in your hands lies my destiny, so help me to take hold of your hand and not reject you. Sometimes I feel that you have let go of me, yet in deep truth I know it is not you who has let go, but I who have done so. Help me, Lord, take heart in what you say and place me and my future in your hands. It seems that I often fail when I try to take control of my life without your help. It's a hard lesson for me to learn, so I pray that you will protect me from myself and give me strength to keep myself committed to you. Each and every morning, remind me that for today you are committed to me and I to you. This I ask in your name. Amen.

Reflections

I know that I portray false images to others by the masks I wear. Why do I wear masks, and why am I afraid to be myself? What feelings accompany the masks I wear?

What can I do to resolve the "mask wearing" when I am around others?

When I see others wearing masks, what are my feelings about them, and do I see myself in their shoes?

My ultimate goal is to wear no masks. What can I do to obtain that goal?

Regret

John 16:20–23

I tell you truly: you will weep and mourn while the world rejoices; you will grieve for a time, but your grief will be turned into joy. When a woman is in labor she is sad that her time has come. When she has borne her child, she no longer remembers her pain for joy that a man has been born into the world. In the same way, you are sad for a time, but I shall see you again; then your hearts will rejoice with a joy no one can take from you. On that day you will have no questions to ask me. I give you my assurance, whatever you ask the Father, he will give you in my name.

PRAYER/MEDITATION

Heavenly Father, the woman in childbirth calls to mind that she suffered and in suffering brought forth a new life. I, too, have suffered, I, too, can feel new life within, and I, too, should have no regrets. But I find myself looking backward at my past and staying stuck, and not looking forward to what great joy and wonderment you have planned for me. I know the past is over and cannot be changed. Today is here. Help me, Lord, to make the most of it so that I can see in myself and others a new life without regrets. Amen.

Reflections

Dwelling on past hurts can only be demeaning and harmful to your growth. How can you learn to accept the past as past and put more effort on today?

"Today is the first day of the rest of your life." What is the meaning of this for you?

God said he wants us to have life and have it to the fullest. We cannot have life to the fullest if we are bogged down in bad memories or regrets of the past. Forgiveness is the way to rid yourself of these encumbrances. Can you forgive and forget, so that you can enjoy new life? Why or why not?

God has given you the gift of time. How can you take advantage of the time he has given you to lay aside your past without regret, and to forgive rather than retain the resentment?

The Sweat Shirt Game

Philippians 4:8–9

Finally, my brothers, your thoughts should be wholly directed to all that is true, all that deserves respect, all that is honest, pure, admirable, decent, virtuous, or worthy of praise. Live according to what you have learned and accepted, what you have heard me say and seen me do. Then will the God of peace be with you.

PRAYER/MEDITATION

O my loving Jesus, sometimes I feel dissatisfied with who I am. I feel insecure and I am afraid to let others know the real me. I know that I can love others. I know that others accept me. Yet I feel that this is not enough. I feel that society demands that I be more than I am, and this causes me to hide behind a mask and be untruthful. Lord, help me to see myself as you see me. I know that the gifts and talents you have given me may not be the ones that the world places a high value on, but they are the gifts you have given me to share with others. So help me to share my gifts and talents with others. This I ask in your name. Amen.

Reflections

How do you feel when you find out that people have misrepresented themselves to you?

How do others perceive you when you display to them a different person than the person you really are?

Can real friendships be built on misrepresentations? What kind of troubles can arise?

Honesty is at the top of the lists of characteristics most desired by others. Are you honest about who you are when you present yourself to others?

Read 2 Corinthians 12:9–10, and reflect on how that should affect you and how you live.

Self-Esteem

Philippians 4:11–13

I do not say this because I am in want, for whatever the situation I find myself in, I have learned to be self-sufficient. I am experienced in being brought low, yet I know what it is to have an abundance. I have learned how to cope with every circumstance—how to eat well or go hungry, to be well provided for or do without. In him who is the source of my strength I have strength for everything.

PRAYER/MEDITATION

Almighty God, I ask you with my whole heart and soul, mind and body, to share with me the greatness you have created in me. Help me see the value I have within that you have so graciously given me. Help me to regain as much confidence in myself as you have in me. Lord, you are my strength and my power. Grant me the vision to know that your presence is in me now and forever. That is all I will ever need. Amen.

Reflections

How do you feel about the statement, "God doesn't make junk"?
How can you come to know your gifts, talents, and abilities?
List all of your virtues, even if they need more development.

Make a list of the virtues that you think you would like to have. What would you have to do to obtain these virtues?

How will you thank God for the good things he has given you? How do you ask for his help to obtain the things you want to become?

Self-Growth

John 14:16–21

I will ask the Father and he will give you another Paraclete to be with you always: the Spirit of truth, whom the world cannot accept, since it neither sees him nor recognizes him; but you can recognize him because he remains with you and will be within you. I will not leave you orphaned; I will come back to you. A little while now and the world will see me no more; but you see me as one who has life, and you will have life. On that day you will know that I am in my Father, and you in me, and I in you. He who obeys the commandments he has from me is the man who loves me; and he who loves me will be loved by my Father. I too will love him and reveal myself to him.

PRAYER/MEDITATION

O Holy Spirit, you are my protector, my teacher, my inspiration; help me in my time of need. Reveal yourself to me so that I can know and serve you better. Show me God's will and help me to accept his will with an open heart. Help me to understand God's word and show me where to begin so that I can realize the true meaning of life and do the things God expects me to do. For this I pray, through Christ our Lord. Amen.

Reflections

"He must increase, while I must decrease" (John 3:30). How can you put this into action in your own life? (Be specific.)

Jesus said to him, "Stand up! Pick up your mat and walk" (John 5:8). What does this say or mean to you?

What areas in your life do you feel are empty and in what areas would you like to grow? (Identify the feelings, good and bad.)

If you desire self-growth, how can you learn it better than through the word of God? Are you ready and prepared to grow? What are the changes you will be required to make?

Resentment

Do not judge, and you will not be judged. Do not condemn, and you will not be condemned. Pardon, and you shall be pardoned. Give, and it shall be given to you; a good measure, pressed down, shaken together, running over, will they pour into the fold of your garment. For the measure you measure with will be measured back to you.

PRAYER/MEDITATION

Lord God, our heavenly Father, I try to love as you love and to forgive as you forgive, yet I find it such a struggle. I know if I hold resentment, I only reject love and forgiveness. In the prayer that you taught us, we ask you to forgive us our trespasses as we forgive those who trespass against us. So I ask you, Lord, to forgive me and teach me to forgive and let go of my resentments toward others. I do not want to separate myself from you. So help me to look to the future that I know I have in your love. Help me to forgive as you have forgiven me, and to know that my strength is in you. This I ask through Christ our Lord. Amen.

Reflections

What can I do to understand that the kingdom of God is in the present, not the past or the future?

What can I do to let go of the resentment I feel?

Do I want to be forgiven in the same manner that I forgive others?

How can I reconcile with those who resent me?

Spiritual Growth

God's Love

1 John 4:7–13

Beloved, let us love one another because love is of God; everyone who loves is begotten of God and has knowledge of God. The man without love has known nothing of God, for God is love. God's love was revealed in our midst in this way: he sent his only Son to the world that we might have life through him. Love, then, consists in this: not that we have loved God but that he has loved us and has sent his Son as an offering for our sins. Beloved, if God has loved us so, we must have the same love for one another. No one has ever seen God. Yet if we love one another, God dwells in us, and his love is brought to perfection in us. The way we know we remain in him and he in us is that he has given us of his Spirit.

PRAYER/MEDITATION

My loving God, I know that when I love others and share your love with all who surround me, it is then that I am the happiest. And you tell us it is possible. So I know that I am the one who keeps us apart. But it is hard being human, and it is hard to love unconditionally, as you do. You know my weakness and you know that I get angry and do not follow your example. So give me your strength and your grace, Lord, so that I may learn to love others as you have loved us. For this I pray, through Christ our Lord. Amen.

Reflections

You know you feel good when you do good things for others. What can you do to become more aware of this, and what can you do for others?

Remember an incident when you did something nice for someone. Reflect on how you felt and how it made the other person feel.

Unconditional love is difficult for many of us to accomplish, yet it is what God expects of us. What steps can you take to achieve this for yourself?

"Love is not love until it is given away." What does this mean to you, and how can you adopt this idea in your own life?

Disappointment

Matthew 26:69-74

Peter was sitting in the courtyard when one of the serving girls came over to him and said, "You too were with Jesus the Galilean." He denied it in front of everyone: "I do not know what you are talking about!" When he went out to the gate another girl saw him and said to those nearby, "This man was with Jesus the Nazorean." Again he denied it with an oath: "I do not know the man!" A little while later some bystanders came over to Peter and said, "You are certainly one of them! Even your accent gives you away!" At that he began cursing, and swore, "I do not even know the man!"

PRAYER/MEDITATION

Lord Jesus, I take refuge in your words, but I find myself holding onto the disappointments in my life. I drift back in time and dwell on them, saving them as though they were important and my life depended on them. I know this is foolish, so I ask for your strength to help me let go and to love and forgive those who have disappointed me. I know you have also known disappointments, in your apostles and in me, but you overcame all with love and forgiveness. Help me, Lord, to overcome the disappointments in my life. Help me to see them as opportunities to learn more about you, to accept them as you have, and to turn them into love and forgiveness of others. Amen.

Reflections

How disappointed Jesus must have felt with Peter! How do you react when faced with disappointments?

James, John, and other disciples of Jesus also disappointed him, but Jesus demonstrated understanding and forgiveness by washing their feet. How can you demonstrate understanding and forgiveness to those who have disappointed you?

How can you turn your disappointments around and learn from them?

Can you see your disappointments as opportunities to love and forgive others?

Christian Living

James 2:14–26

My brothers, what good is it to profess faith without practicing it? Such faith has no power to save one, has it? If a brother or sister has nothing to wear and no food for the day and you say to them, "Good-bye and good luck! Keep warm and well fed," but do not meet their bodily needs, what good is that? So it is with the faith that does nothing in practice. It is thoroughly lifeless.

To such a person one might say, "You have faith and I have works—is that it?" Show me your faith without works, and I will show you the faith that underlies my works! Do you believe that God is one? You are quite right. The demons believe that and shudder. Do you want proof, you ignoramus, that without works faith is idle? Was not our father Abraham justified by his works when he offered his son Isaac on the altar? There you see proof that faith was both assisting his works and implemented by his works. You also see how the scripture was fulfilled which says, "Abraham believed God, and it was credited to him as justice"; for this he received the title "God's friend."

You must perceive that a person is justified by his works and not by faith alone. Rahab the harlot will illustrate the point. Was she not justified by her works when she harbored the messengers and sent them out by a different route? Be assured, then, that faith without works is as dead as a body without breath.

PRAYER/MEDITATION

Lord, in the letter of James you tell us how we are to live as Christians. I am aware that I do not always live a Christian lifestyle. I fall short on those things that I should do and do some of the things I should not. Lord, give me some guidance and show me the way. Come into my life and help me to take control. Give me the endurance St. James speaks of. Help me to control my tongue and restrain my feelings. Help me not to judge others, and teach me not only to know what is right but to practice it in everything I do. And, most of all, be with me, Lord, so that I can become strong in both mind and spirit. Amen.

Reflections

How do your shortcomings compare to traits you dislike or experience in others?

How can you forgive the shortcomings of yourself and others?

List your shortcomings in leading a Christian life. Taking one a day, make a plan to overcome each one.

How does God forgive you and how do you accept God's forgiveness?

What does it mean to you to be a Christian?

Love

John 3:16–17

Yes, God so loved the world that he gave his only Son, that whoever believes in him may not die but may have eternal life. God did not send the Son into the world to condemn the world, but that the world might be saved through him.

PRAYER/MEDITATION

Loving Father, you love us so much that you created us in your image and likeness. Then you gave us your Son, Jesus Christ, to show us how to love. And he gave up his life so that we might have life everlasting.

You know me better then I know myself. You want me to have nothing less than eternal salvation. But, Lord, you know my weaknesses and you know my inability to love as you love. Show me how I can return the love that you have given me. I accept your love and I struggle with what you ask of me—to love my enemies, to forgive seventy times seven. In this I must ask for more guidance. I am humbled at my inability to do your will, so please, Lord, grant me the grace necessary to be a good Samaritan and grant me the ability to accept others as you do. Help me to see you, Lord, in everyone, and perhaps then I can learn to love all as you have loved us. I ask this through Christ our Lord. Amen.

Reflections

Make a list of the people who love you, and then make a list of the people you love. Which list is longer? Why is it that way?

Whom would you like to add to your list?

What can you do to increase the number of people on both lists?

How can you return to others the love God has shown for you?

"If you love those who love you, what merit is there in that? Do not tax collectors do as much?" (Matthew 5:46). How can you use this thought in your own life?

Talking to God

Psalm 16:1–3, 7–11

Keep me, O God, for in you I take refuge; I say to the Lord, "My Lord are you. Apart from you I have no good." How wonderfully has he made me cherish the holy ones who are in his land! I bless the Lord who counsels me; even in the night my heart exhorts me. I set the Lord ever before me; with him at my right hand I shall not be disturbed. Therefore my heart is glad and my soul rejoices; my body, too, abides in confidence, because you will not abandon my soul to the nether world, nor will you suffer your faithful one to undergo corruption. You will show me the path to life, fullness of joys in your presence, the delights at your right hand forever.

PRAYER/MEDITATION

My Lord, I know you love me more than mothers love their children, yet sometimes I feel that you are not present or at least not available when I call. But yet I know that this is not true. You always hear me. Lord, help me to accept the fact that you are my friend, a loving God who is always at my call. Help me to realize that you are standing next to me when I need you and even when I don't. Let me know that you are as near as my shadow and as close to me as my breath. I can have no secrets from you, so I can tell you everything. Teach me to listen to you and to let go of myself and the barriers that I impose on our relationship. For only then will I be able to hear you more, love you more, serve you more, and know you more. Amen.

Reflections

What is your present image of God?

If you could visibly see God standing in front of you now, what would you say to him or ask him? Then what? After that, what?

Do you feel God's presence next to you most of the time? Explain in detail.

Do you talk to God as if he is your friend or as if he is your boss?

Build a dialogue with God, and let him answer you.

Forgiveness

Forgiveness

Matthew 5:38–48

You have heard the commandment, "An eye for an eye, a tooth for a tooth." But what I say to you is: offer no resistance to injury. When a person strikes you on the right cheek, turn and offer him the other. If anyone wants to go to law over your shirt, hand him your coat as well. Should anyone press you into service for one mile, go with him two miles. Give to the man who begs from you. Do not turn your back on the borrower.

You have heard the commandment, "You shall love your countryman but hate your enemy." My command to you is: love your enemies, pray for your persecutors. This will prove that you are sons of your heavenly Father, for his sun rises on the bad and the good, he rains on the just and the unjust. If you love those who love you, what merit is there in that? Do not tax collectors do as much? And if you greet your brothers only, what is so praiseworthy about that? Do not pagans do as much? In a word, you must be made perfect as your heavenly Father is perfect.

PRAYER/MEDITATION

Jesus, by your words and your actions, you have shown us how to forgive and be forgiving. I often find it hard to start to forgive. Yet I ask that you forgive me even when I am not forgiving of others. Give me the strength to start to forgive others and enough grace to endure. I must start; for you have told us that through forgiveness, we are forgiven. So I call on you, Lord. Help me work through my anger and frustration, and help me want to forgive, so that I will be as forgiving as our heavenly Father is in forgiving us. I ask this in your name. Amen.

Reflections

Forgiving someone who has hurt us is probably the hardest of all things to do, yet God asks this of us. What will it take for you to forgive those who have hurt you? And if that seems impossible, what then?

When God tells us that he will use the same measure for us that we use for others, what is he asking us to do? How will you respond? How do you feel about it?

If you accept God's forgiveness and then do not forgive others, how should God react? Explain.

When Christ was crucified he said, "Forgive them, Father! They do not know what they are doing." Can you do the same for those who have crucified you?

Love Your Enemies

Romans 12:19–21

Beloved, do not avenge yourselves; leave that to God's wrath, for it is written: "Vengeance is mine; I will repay, says the Lord." But "if your enemy is hungry, feed him; if he is thirsty, give him something to drink; by doing this you will heap burning coals upon his head." Do not be conquered by evil but conquer evil with good.

PRAYER/MEDITATION

Jesus, when I see how many times and how many ways you showed love for your enemies—those who plotted against you, rejected you, denied you, abandoned you, and those who crucified you—I begin to understand what you mean when you say to love our enemies. I find that it is easier to forgive friends, but it is so hard for me to forgive my enemies. Lord, I know I can forgive, but I need your help. Send me your Spirit, the Spirit of love, endurance, patience, and kindness. Empower me with forgiveness, Lord, so I can love as you have shown us to love. Through Christ Jesus. Amen.

Reflections

Forgiveness is an act of the will. How does this affect you?

The Bible tells us not to pass judgment on others and to work for peace and strengthen one another. How does this relate to your enemies?

"In summary, then, all of you should be like-minded, sympathetic, loving toward one another, kindly disposed, and humble. Do not return evil for evil or insult for insult. Return a blessing instead. This you have been called to do, that you may receive a blessing as your inheritance" (1 Peter 3:8–9). Make a list of those you need to forgive, and outline a plan of action to achieve forgiveness.

"This is how all will know you are my disciples: by your love for one another" (John 13:35). What would it take for you to do to become a disciple for Christ?

"I Wish I Had Said . . ."

Ephesians 4:29–32

Never let evil talk pass your lips; say only the good things men need to hear, things that will really help them. Do nothing to sadden the Holy Spirit with whom you were sealed against the day of redemption. Get rid of all bitterness, all passion and anger, harsh words, slander, and malice of every kind. In place of these, be kind to one another, compassionate, and mutually forgiving, just as God has forgiven you in Christ.

PRAYER/MEDITATION

Dear heavenly Father, it seems so hard to change from my former way of life. My life is full of my history and I seem to keep repeating the past. Help me to forgive those who have hurt me. Show me the way to renew the spiritual way of being. Help me to use holiness to overcome my unforgiving ways. It seems so easy to lash out at people who have hurt me, yet I know that is not your way. I really want to be more Christ-like. I really want to mend and grow into the loving, forgiving person that you want me to be. I accept what you say, and I ask for your grace to do all I can do to receive the joy of the Holy Spirit. Amen.

Reflections

There are two sides to each argument. Can you see the other side of those you disagree with? Can you see why they feel the way they do?

"Never let evil talk pass your lips; say only the good things men need to hear, things that will really help them" (Ephesians 4:29). Examine your conscience and see how your words may be harmful or hurtful to those with whom you speak. List those words and find other words to replace them.

Can I forgive seventy times seven times if necessary?

I ask God for forgiveness of my trespasses and accept his forgiveness. Can I also learn to forgive others as God has forgiven me?

Do You Enjoy Hating?

Psalm 25:4–10

Your ways, O Lord, make known to me; teach me your paths. Guide me in your truth and teach me, for you are God my savior, and for you I wait all the day. Remember that your compassion, O Lord, and your kindness are from of old. The sins of my youth and my frailties remember not; in your kindness remember me because of your goodness, O Lord. Good and upright is the Lord; thus he shows sinners the way. He guides the humble to justice, he teaches the humble his way. All the paths of the Lord are kindness and constancy toward those who keep his covenant and his decrees.

PRAYER/MEDITATION

Dear loving God, anger, hatred, and unforgiving ways can take the life out of my soul. When I am angry I do not feel your presence. The hatred takes over and destroys me. Lord God, grant me the grace and strength to put the anger and hate behind me. They have no place in heaven or on earth. Guide me, cleanse my soul, rid my mind of these evil thoughts before they consume me. Then fill the voids within me with only love for all, and inspire me to love and forgive as you have loved and forgiven me. This I ask in your name. Amen.

Reflections

"Hatred stirs up disputes, but love covers all offenses" (Proverbs 10:12). How can you put this into practice in your own life?

If hatred keeps you in the dark and consumes your life, what must you do to change this? Make a plan to accomplish this.

"If anyone says, 'My love is fixed on God,' yet hates his brother, he is a liar. One who has no love for the brother he has seen cannot love the God he has not seen" (1 John 4:20). Is this you, or what you have or may become? How can you change?

Hatred only hurts the one who hates. The person being hated cannot feel the anger, the increased heart rate, the adrenaline, the stress, or the tension. Can you imagine the devastating effects this has on your physical well-being?

Remember a time when you have felt forgiven. How did it feel? Explain how and why.

How Can I Learn To Forgive?

Luke 6:27–32

To you who hear me, I say: Love your enemies, do good to those who hate you; bless those who curse you and pray for those who maltreat you. When someone slaps you on one cheek, turn and give him the other; when someone takes your coat, let him have your shirt as well. Give to all who beg from you. When a man takes what is yours, do not demand it back. Do to others what you would have them do to you. If you love those who love you, what credit is that to you? Even sinners love those who love them.

PRAYER/MEDITATION

God, Father of light, open my eyes to your love; give me the strength to see past my prejudices and opinions of others. Remove the barriers that prevent me from loving others as you have loved me. It is not easy for me to forgive those who trespass against me. Yet you find it in your heart to forgive me. So, Lord, give me the strength to forgive others, so that I may know that the only way to true happiness is through your love. Fill my heart with forgiveness, inspire me with your grace and your love, and let me feel the goodness and the peace that can only come through you. This I ask through Christ our Lord. Amen.

Reflections

Forgiveness must come from your desire to forgive. What must you do to find that desire within yourself?

God knows what is in your heart. Now is the time you can start to forgive those who have hurt you. What can you forgive today? Tomorrow? Next week?

Remember a time when you helped someone in need. Remember how you felt. It feels just as good when you have forgiven someone. Whom can you forgive?

Love, peace of mind, and trust are all results of forgiveness. Hate, anger, mistrust, and anxiety are all results of an unwillingness to forgive. Which do you choose?

Sexuality

Sexual Attitudes

Jude 20–22

But you, beloved, grow strong in your holy faith through prayer in the Holy Spirit. Persevere in God's love, and welcome the mercy of our Lord Jesus Christ which leads to life eternal. Correct those who are confused; the others you must rescue, snatching them from the fire.

PRAYER/MEDITATION

Heavenly Father, having a healthy and holy attitude toward sex seems difficult in our society today. We are faced with a society which largely reduces human sexuality to the level of something commonplace and links it solely with the body and selfish pleasure. Help me to recognize that sex and sexuality are beautiful gifts from you. Being from you, show me, Lord, how to use these gifts properly and in keeping with your intent. Guide my feelings and help me not to misuse these gifts you have given to me. Strengthen me in my acceptance that sexuality is an enrichment of the whole person—body, emotions and soul—and let it manifest itself in leading us to the gift of self in love. I pray for strength, grace, and guidance to learn to love as you love. And this I ask in Christ's name. Amen.

Reflections

Define the difference between sexuality, sexual identity, and genital sexuality. How do you feel each one of these plays a role in your life?

Although we are sexual beings, that does not mean that we are necessarily sexually active. How do you see yourself?

Some people say that sexual intercourse between consenting adults hurts no one. Consider each one of the following: lack of bonding, sex used for self-gratification only, guilt, and lack of respect for the other person. Explain each in detail.

We are custodians of God's gifts, and thus we must account for our use of these gifts. How would you explain to Christ how you have used the gifts that God has given you?

Single Again—What Is My Attitude About Sex?

1 Corinthians 3:16–20

Are you not aware that you are the temple of God, and that the Spirit of God dwells in you? If anyone destroys God's temple, God will destroy him. For the temple of God is holy, and you are that temple.

Let no one delude himself. If anyone of you thinks he is wise in a worldly way, he had better become a fool. In that way he will really be wise, for the wisdom of this world is absurdity with God. Scripture says, "He catches the wise in their craftiness"; and again, "The Lord knows how empty are the thoughts of the wise."

PRAYER/MEDITATION

Lord Jesus, I feel weak and weary, and I ask you to give me the strength and courage to understand that this too will pass. My world has been turned around and I do not know which direction to proceed. I am alone and need your love. I ask you, Lord, to give me guidance. You are my source of strength, my courage and my light. Help me to understand that I do not need sex to feel loved, and that it is more important to give love than to receive it in misleading ways. I ask for your forgiveness for all my transgressions, and I place myself in your hands to hold me and form me in your image. Open me to the truth and strengthen me with your words that I may live in your Spirit and have true love for all. Amen.

Reflections

Do you see any disagreement in what you have been taught about sex and the Bible's teachings on sex? If so, what?

What does the Bible say about worldly knowledge and its worth to you? Explain how you feel about this.

Sexuality and sex are both gifts from God. Does this mean you can exercise your freedom of choice with sex and sexuality?

"What I say to you is: anyone who looks lustfully at a woman has already committed adultery with her in his thoughts" (Matthew 5:28). This also applies to a woman who looks at a man. What was Christ saying, and how does this apply to your life, your feelings and your values?

Sexual Conduct

James 4:1–6

Where do the conflicts and disputes among you originate? Is it not your inner cravings that make war within your members? What you desire you do not obtain, and so you resort to murder. You envy and you cannot acquire, so you quarrel and fight. You do not obtain because you do not ask. You ask and you do not receive because you ask wrongly, with a view to squandering what you receive on your pleasures. O you unfaithful ones, are you not aware that love of the world is enmity to God? A man is marked out as God's enemy if he chooses to be the world's friend. Do you suppose it is to no purpose that scripture says, "The spirit he has implanted in us tends toward jealousy"? Yet he bestows a greater gift, for the sake of which it is written, "God resists the proud but bestows his favor on the lowly."

PRAYER/MEDITATION

Heavenly Father, the world and its values confuse and consume me. I realize that when I ask for things that are for my personal self-gratification, I am not thinking of others, only of my own selfish pleasures. Therefore, Lord, I ask that you teach me to pray for those things in life which will help me to grow in your strength and wisdom. Teach me your values and your will. Teach me how to open my mind and my heart to these values so that they may take precedence in my life. And I pray that through my struggles you will be patient with me, for I have much to learn. These things I ask in Jesus' name. Amen.

Reflections

Clyde C. Besson says in his book *Picking Up the Pieces* that there are ten levels of intimacy, the tenth being general intimacy. What does general intimacy mean to you?

What were the last ten things you prayed for? Can you identify them as need of the higher things or greed for the worldly things?

How do you think people who are chaste live happily?

How do you think the values of the opposite sex correspond to your values about sex and sexuality? What do you think are the differences and how do they compare to yours?

Trust

Trusting

Psalm 9:1–4, 8–11

I will give thanks to you, O Lord, with all my heart; I will declare all your wondrous deeds. I will be glad and exult in you; I will sing praise to your name, Most High, because my enemies are turned back, overthrown and destroyed before you. But the Lord sits enthroned forever; he has set up his throne for judgment. He judges the world with justice; he governs the peoples with equity. The Lord is a stronghold for the oppressed, a stronghold in times of distress. They trust in you who cherish your name, for you forsake not those who seek you, O Lord.

PRAYER/MEDITATION

Dear heavenly Father, I am trying so hard to learn to trust again, but my efforts seem to be in vain. Help to restore in me, Lord, that feeling of trusting others. And restore in me the trust I need to become a normal and loving person. Please help me to put away those experiences that caused me to lose trust in others. I am reminded in Mark's gospel of the father of the boy possessed where he also cried out, "I do believe; help my lack of trust." Father, I know that it is your desire that we have trust in you, and I do believe in you, and deep inside of me I have faith and trust in you. So, God, I pray that you grace me with your love and guide the spirit of trust within me so that I may again love, forgive, and trust others. Amen.

Reflections

What is preventing you from trusting? What can you do to help yourself become a trusting person again?

Examine all the negatives you feel about trusting. Then list all the good feelings that come with trust. Is it worth it to punish yourself and deny yourself all the positive feelings that come with trust?

Harboring ill feelings only hurts you. If you can forgive others you can learn to trust again. What must you do to forgive?

How can you take God's examples of forgiveness and trust and empower yourself to trust others?

```
Baptist Book Store  #4689
Southern Baptist Seminary
   2825 Lexington Road
  Louisville, KY  40280
  (502)897-4506

CLERK      3
REGISTER   4
RECEIPT # 8900015970
DATE      02/22/94
TIME      11:20 AM

  ISBN/SPCN    PRICE QUANTITY AMOUNT
  9990231389    2.98      1    2.98
     SUPPLIES DEPARTMENT


               SUB TOTAL    2.98
  SALES TAX ON 2.98 @ 6.000   .18
             GRAND TOTAL    3.16
          PAID WITH CASH    3.20
           CHANGE RECVD      .04

Please keep your receipt. Exchanges and
returns honored within 2 weeks of sale.
```

Being Single

Psalm 25:14–18

The friendship of the Lord is with those who fear him, and his covenant, for their instruction. My eyes are ever toward the Lord, for he will free my feet from the snare. Look toward me, and have pity on me, for I am alone and afflicted. Relieve the troubles of my heart, and bring me out of my distress. Put an end to my affliction and my suffering, and take away all my sins.

PRAYER/MEDITATION

Jesus, being single seems to be out of sync with the rest of society, but you above all must know how I feel. For you it was a call from the Father; for me it is not. Lord, be my strength to face life and go on. Help me to find harmony in life, and to find peace with society and myself. Guide me, Lord, to accept myself as a whole person and to rely on those friends and relatives with whom you have blessed me. I thank you for all the blessings you have bestowed on me. Open up my eyes that I may once again see the beauty that surrounds me by your presence. Open up my ears that I may hear your voice. And open up my mind that I may see good in all your children. Amen.

Reflections

Make a list of support people you have and categorize the type of support you can count on from each.

What kind of support do you think you need beyond that which you have?

When the kind of support you feel you need is not readily available, what must you do, and where do you go?

"Christ's peace must reign in your hearts, since as members of the one body you have been called to that peace. Dedicate yourselves to thankfulness" (Colossians 3:15). Explain and meditate on how you can accept peace.

Seeking Support

Psalm 91:1–4, 9–16

You who dwell in the shelter of the Most High, who abide in the shadow of the Almighty, say to the Lord, "My refuge and my fortress, my God, in whom I trust."

For he will rescue you from the snare of the fowler, from the destroying pestilence. With his pinions he will cover you, and under his wings you shall take refuge; his faithfulness is a buckler and a shield.

Because you have the Lord for your refuge, you have made the Most High your stronghold. No evil shall befall you, nor shall affliction come near your tent. For to his angels he has given command about you, that they guard you in all your ways. Upon their hands they shall bear you up, lest you dash your foot against a stone. You shall tread upon the asp and the viper; you shall trample down the lion and the dragon. Because he clings to me, I will deliver him; I will set him on high because he acknowledges my name. He shall call upon me, and I will answer him; I will be with him in distress; I will deliver him and glorify him; with length of days I will gratify him and will show him my salvation.

PRAYER/MEDITATION

Almighty God and Father, I know that you will never abandon me. I know that you are always with me and I know that you reveal your gifts through others. So I turn to the friends that you have given me, but I find it hard to share my pain with them. So help me, Lord, to accept support from others openly and with love. Grant me the strength to turn to others for the support that I need, and the grace to accept that support. Be with me while I grow in your love, and grant to me the ability to be an instrument of your peace. This I ask through Christ our Lord. Amen.

Reflections

How do you feel when you receive support from others?

God tells us that the greatest commandment is to love God and to love our neighbors as ourselves. What must we do to fulfill this commandment?

Think of a time when someone really helped support you when you needed it, and think of a time when you gave support to someone else who needed it. How did it make you feel?

What can you do to voluntarily give support to others? What kind of support can you offer? (blood center, Big Brothers, Scouts, lay ministry, church, support groups, etc.)

Trust in Self

Sirach 2:2–9

Be sincere of heart and steadfast, undisturbed in time of adversity. Cling to him, forsake him not; thus will your future be great. Accept whatever befalls you, in crushing misfortune be patient. For in fire gold is tested, and worthy men in the crucible of humiliation. Trust God and he will help you; make straight your ways and hope in him. You who fear the Lord, wait for his mercy; turn not away lest you fall. You who fear the Lord, trust him, and your reward will not be lost. You who fear the Lord, hope for good things, for lasting joy and mercy.

PRAYER/MEDITATION

My Father in heaven, fill me with the message of Sirach, for in my confusion I call on you. O Lord, lift me up with the spirit of trust—trust in you, trust in others, and trust in myself. My wounds are fresh and the pain is deep. And I know my healing can only begin in you. I know I must trust in you so that I may overcome the pain and humiliation I feel. Help me, O Lord, to accept life, the good and the bad. Give me the strength I will need and the patience to endure the pain I often feel. Plant the seeds of faith, hope and love in me and see that they flourish. I believe in you, Lord, and I know you will not forsake me, for you are compassionate and merciful. Amen.

Reflections

Jesus died to save us. Why was it so important for him to save us?

Since you are a child of God, do you really trust in God?

Trusting in God means that you trust in yourself as a child of God. Write about this connection.

If the Spirit of the Lord is within us, do you listen and trust what the Spirit is telling you?

You have a free will; therefore trust is an act of your free will. How can you put this into daily practice?

Stages of Trust

Jeremiah 1:4–9

The word of the Lord came to me thus: Before I formed you in the womb I knew you, before you were born I dedicated you, a prophet to the nations I appointed you. "Ah, Lord God!" I said, "I know not how to speak. I am too young." But the Lord answered me, Say not, "I am too young." To whomever I send you, you shall go; whatever I command you, you shall speak. Have no fear before them, because I am with you to deliver you, says the Lord. Then the Lord extended his hand and touched my mouth, saying, See, I place my words in your mouth!

PRAYER/MEDITATION

Almighty Father, I have so far to go on my journey to wholeness. I count on you, O Lord, to strengthen me on my path. I lack the knowledge and wisdom necessary to go very far. Take my hand, Lord, lead me on your path to holiness, and empower me with your wisdom to make the right decisions that I face daily. Sometimes I just don't know what is best for me. At these times I feel bogged down in despair. I need your wisdom because I am overwhelmed in what others say I should do. Guide me and bless me. Speak to me when I call out to you. Be with me, Lord, in all that I do. Lead me through the paths of righteousness to the wholeness that you have designed for me. Amen

Reflections

Do you count or rely on anyone else to make you happy? If so, why? If not, why not?

God created all of us, gave each of us certain gifts (talents, abilities, intelligence), and promised us that with him it is enough. Do you agree? Disagree? Why? How do you see yourself? How do you see your status in life? Is it enough?

To what extent are you motivated in your decision by other people's expectations of you? If greatly affected, why? If not affected, why not?

"I am content with weaknesses, insults, hardships, persecutions, and difficulties for Christ's sake. For when I am weak, then I am strong" (2 Corinthians 12:10). How does that fit your life?

Feelings

Isaiah 35:3–7

Strengthen the hands that are feeble, make firm the knees that are weak. Say to those whose hearts are frightened: Be strong, fear not! Here is your God, he comes with vindication; with divine recompense he comes to save you. Then will the eyes of the blind be opened, the ears of the deaf be cleared. Then will the lame leap like a stag, then the tongue of the dumb will sing. Streams will burst forth in the desert and rivers in the steppe. The burning sands will become pools, and the thirsty ground, springs of water. The abode where jackals lurk will be a marsh for the reed and papyrus.

PRAYER/MEDITATION

Lord, I find it hard to share my feelings with others. I am afraid to admit to anyone that I have some of the feelings that I have; I think that if they knew, they might think less of me. Yet it is almost unbearable to hold those feelings within me. I know that you are listening, and I know that you know how I feel. But I need others to put their hand on my shoulder and tell me that it's going to be all right and that they understand. Feelings are such a personal thing to me. Give me the ability to share my feeling with others, and give them the gift of understanding. I call upon you, my Lord, for help and assistance. Send me a dear friend in whom I can trust. In Christ's name I pray. Amen.

Reflections

What feelings are you afraid to expose to others? Why?

There have been times in your life that you have shared feelings with someone. How did it feel? Is it different now? What can you do to resolve the problem?

Friendships are built on mutual trust, forgiveness, and love for one another. Whom do you trust or distrust? Whom have you forgiven or not forgiven? Can you become a trusted and forgiving friend to others? What does it take?

You cannot control your feelings; you can only control how you manage them. List the problem feelings and plan on how you are going to manage them.

Sometimes I Need a Friend

Sirach 51:6–12

I was at the point of death, my soul was nearing the depths of the nether world. I turned every way, but there was no one to help me, I looked for one to sustain me, but could find no one. But then I remembered the mercies of the Lord, his kindness through ages past. For he saves those who take refuge in him, and rescues them from every evil. So I raised my voice from the very earth, from the gates of the nether world, my cry. I called out: O Lord, you are my Father, you are my champion and my savior. Do not abandon me in time of trouble, in the midst of storms and dangers. I will ever praise your name and be constant in my prayers to you. Thereupon the Lord heard my voice, he listened to my appeal. He saved me from evil of every kind and preserved me in time of trouble. For this reason I thank him and I praise him; I bless the name of the Lord.

PRAYER/MEDITATION

Dear Father, I know that you want what is best for me and that your plans for me contain peace and love. I know also that you will change my life for the better. But, Lord, I need you and I need friends that I can count on—friends that are not judgmental or condemning, friends that are ready to support and accept me just where I am. I pray, Lord, for your help, that I may accept support from others. Allow me to be open to them and the support that they can give me. Fill me with your peace and love and grant us all the power to give support to others in their hour of need. Amen.

Reflections

Think of the best friend you ever had. What did you see in that person that made him or her your best friend?

You cannot do anything so bad that Jesus cannot forgive you. Can you forgive your friends the way Jesus forgives us? What about those who are not your friends?

Many times the lack of forgiving oneself blocks or is a barrier to being able to forgive others. Can you think of a time when this has happened to you? Did you overcome it? What were the steps that you took?

To get support or to give support means that you accept or are accepted just the way you are. Is it easy for you to accept others without being judgmental?

Parenting

Parenting

Matthew 18:1-5

Just then the disciples came up to Jesus with the question, "Who is of greatest importance in the kingdom of God?" He called a little child over and stood him in their midst and said: "I assure you, unless you change and become like little children, you will not enter the kingdom of God. Whoever makes himself lowly, becoming like this child, is of greatest importance in that heavenly reign. Whoever welcomes one such child for my sake welcomes me."

PRAYER/MEDITATION

Heavenly Father, my children are the greatest gift that you have given me. Hold them in the palm of your hand and protect them from the violence that surrounds them in this world we live in. The Bible tells us how Jesus loved and protected the children. I pray that I can be more like Jesus. Guide me in my responsibilities to my children and show me how to teach my children the way of our Lord Jesus Christ. Give me the knowledge and patience to guide them through the paths of righteousness so that they will grow in your ways. Help me to teach them to be responsible and loving. Children truly are a gift and a blessing from you, Lord, so I pray that I may always treat them as such and guide them to your love. Inspire me, teach me and empower me to the right ways of parenting. These things I ask through Christ our Lord. Amen.

Reflections

Children are often confused and guilt-ridden in accepting the loss of a parent. What can you do to help eliminate and protect your children from these feelings?

Children have two birth parents and they love both. Do you enhance the feeling of loyalty and dedication to the missing parent?

Usually the most stable and reliable children are never confronted with less than the love of both parents. How can you enhance those feelings that truly express love?

How can you teach and inspire your children not to accept what they feel as blame?

Single Parenting

Mark 9:35–37

So he sat down and called the twelve around him and said, "If anyone wishes to rank first, he must remain the last one of all and the servant of all." Then he took a little child, stood him in their midst, and putting his arms around him, said to them, "Whoever welcomes a child such as this for my sake welcomes me. And whoever welcomes me welcomes, not me, but him who sent me."

PRAYER/MEDITATION

Loving Jesus, I thank you for the gift of your love and care that you have shown me and my children. And I thank you for the people you have sent me to be my friends and who also have shown love and care to me. Give me the strength to help my children sort out some of the confused, lonely and angry feelings that often accompany the changes that take place in their lives. Help me to help them recognize their own worth and to show them signs of hope through personal reconciliation and forgiveness. Help us both to be aware of the good qualities that still exist within a single-parent family. And help us, Lord, to grow and learn through the many changes in our family life and our relationship. Amen.

Reflections

(WIDOWED) What can you do to nurture the feelings your children have toward the missing parent?

(DIVORCED) What can you do to keep your children from taking sides between your former spouse and yourself?

Do you accept your children's feelings for the absent parent?

When seemingly insurmountable problems with your children arise, whom or where can you seek help and guidance?

How can you insure for your children a healthy role model for both sexes?

Thoughts on Single Parenting

Mark 10:13–16

People were bringing their little children to him to have him touch them, but the disciples were scolding them for this. Jesus became indignant when he noticed it and said to them: "Let the children come to me and do not hinder them. It is to just such as these that the kingdom of God belongs. I assure you that whoever does not accept the reign of God like a little child shall not take part in it." Then he embraced them and blessed them, placing his hands on them.

PRAYER/MEDITATION

Dear Lord, let me never forget that the kingdom of heaven belongs to those who are humble and pure like children. As I grow older the world seems less personal and more materialistic. I often wonder if it is me, or whether it is just the fact that as I get older, I view the world from a different perspective. Lord, help me to let go and become more child-like; then show me how I can more effectively share Christian values with my children. Help me to develop and engage my child's mind, heart, and soul into knowing that God is a loving Father who wants us to return his love and share it with neighbors, friends, and family. I ask this for my children through your Son, Jesus Christ. Amen.

Reflections

The values we have are well set in our minds. Is it wise to impose our values on our children? why or why not?

As a single parent your time is probably overburdened now. What do you do to assure your children of some individual quality time?

How do you teach your children that God loves them totally when they see things that you and God have not provided for them?

What do moral values mean to you, and how can you effectively establish moral values in your children?

Single Parenting Problems

1 Corinthians 13:4–7

Love is patient; love is kind. Love is not jealous, it does not put on airs, it is not snobbish. Love is never rude, it is not self-seeking, it is not prone to anger; neither does it brood over injuries. Love does not rejoice in what is wrong but rejoices with the truth. There is no limit to love's forbearance, to its trust, its hope, its power to endure.

PRAYER/MEDITATION

O heavenly Father, I know that my children are going through great transitions in their lives and that there are some strong emotions that they are dealing with now. Help me to guide them through this time in their lives without getting ill-mannered and irritable. I know that there is a generation gap that stands between us. And I know that I love my children deeply but at times I find it hard to be patient and kind. So I ask you, Lord, to give me the strength and patience so that I may gain a better understanding of my children's view of the world in which we live. And help them, Lord, to grow in your strength and wisdom, so that we may together find happiness in your truth. Amen.

Reflections

Your thirteen year old child has come to you, devastated because he or she has been rejected by a school group which he or she wanted so much to be a part of. What will you tell him or her?

How would you explain to your child who has just broken up with a "first love" that all is not ended, that there will be others?

Remember a time when your children felt devastated. How did you help them deal with that feeling?

Place yourself at the "pearly gate" and answer the question St. Peter puts to you: "How did you express love to your children, and how did you show them the love of God for all his people on earth?"

Special Problems

How Would You Handle This?

1 Corinthians 12:4–11

There are different gifts but the same Spirit; there are different ministries but the same Lord; there are different works but the same God who accomplishes all of them in everyone. To each person the manifestation of the Spirit is given for the common good. To one the Spirit gives wisdom in discourse, to another the power to express knowledge. Through the Spirit one receives faith; by the same Spirit another is given the gift of healing, and still another miraculous powers. Prophecy is given to one, to another power to distinguish one spirit from another. One receives the gift of tongues, another that of interpreting the tongues. But it is one and the same Spirit who produces all these gifts, distributing them to each as he wills.

PRAYER/MEDITATION

Our Father, I know that you have given each one of us different gifts. And you have given each one of us the power to use these gifts as we choose. So I pray that you give me the ability to choose wisely. Take away the struggle that I often face. Help me to help those who suffer with emotional pain in a caring way. Help me to use my gifts to assist those who are in need. Help me to look beyond my own selfish goals and reach out to others with my time and talents. Help me to teach others to accept one another as they are with their own individual gifts. And guide me, Lord, so that as I reach out to others I may reflect your love and concern for all of us. These things I sincerely ask of you. Amen.

Reflections

What are the gifts that God has given you that you can use to help others?

Using your time and talents, how can you best assist others in their time of need?

"Do unto others as you would have them do unto you." If someone had recently lost a spouse, how would you help them grieve through the loss?

Are there any issues that you would have trouble helping someone work through? What issues are they? Why would you have problems with these issues?

Where Do I Fit In?

Matthew 5:21–24

You have heard the commandment imposed on your forefathers, "You shall not commit murder; every murderer shall be liable to judgment." What I say to you is: everyone who grows angry with his brother shall be liable to judgment; any man who uses abusive language toward his brother shall be answerable to the Sanhedrin, and if he holds him in contempt he risks the fires of Gehenna. If you bring your gift to the altar and there recall that your brother has anything against you, leave your gift at the altar, go first to be reconciled with your brother, and then come and offer your gift.

PRAYER/MEDITATION

I love you, Lord; you are my strength and my protection. Let your Spirit dwell within me and direct my every move. Protect me from the evil that is present in this world, and at the same time give me the courage to step out, risk, and not be afraid. Help me to not mask my feelings with false frowns or smiles, but to be open and honest with others. Help me to show them your love by being a reflection of your Son, Jesus Christ. And fill me, Lord, with compassion for others so that my hand reaches out to help and gives glory and praise to your name. Amen.

Reflections

What is this reading from Matthew telling us?

What must you do to show others the love of God without overpowering them?

What can you do for others to help them find a deeper relationship with Christ?

How can you help ease the hurt and pain of others without being pushy?

Can you stand up for what you believe without feeling defensive or compromising your principles?

With Friends Like This . . .

Colossians 3:12–17

Because you are God's chosen ones, holy and beloved, clothe yourselves with heartfelt mercy, with kindness, humility, meekness, and patience. Bear with one another; forgive whatever grievances you have against one another. Forgive as the Lord has forgiven you. Over all these virtues put on love, which binds the rest together and makes them perfect. Christ's peace must reign in your hearts, since as members of the one body you have been called to that peace. Dedicate yourselves to thankfulness. Let the word of Christ, rich as it is, dwell in you. In wisdom made perfect, instruct and admonish one another. Sing gratefully to God from your hearts in psalms, hymns, and inspired songs. Whatever you do, whether in speech or in action, do it in the name of the Lord Jesus. Give thanks to God the Father through him.

PRAYER/MEDITATION

Lord, fill my spirit with love and compassion so that I can better understand the feelings of others. Help me to understand them without being judgmental. Help me to no longer look at only what is best for me but to consider others and their feelings as well. Light up my path so that I may walk through life guided by your hand and live my life in love, understanding, and harmony with all your people. For then, Lord, I will be surrounded with your peace and serenity to ease the pain and suffering that I have experienced in life. And let that expression of joy that I have found in you be an example for others so that through you all grief and loss can be diminished. In Christ our Lord. Amen.

Reflections

What must you do to become more aware of the feelings of others?

Some people collect stamps, and some people collect coins. What would it take to collect friends? What would you have to do to keep friends? How many could you really maintain? Would it be worth all the work?

What are people really looking for in life?

Other than material things, what do you have that other people want from you?

How much of yourself are you willing to give to others?

Tomorrow

Matthew 6:19–23

Do not lay up for yourselves an earthly treasure. Moths and rust corrode; thieves break in and steal. Make it your practice instead to store up heavenly treasure, which neither moths nor rust corrodes nor thieves break in and steal. Remember, where your treasure is, there your heart is also. The eye is the body's lamp. If your eyes are good, your body will be filled with light; if your eyes are bad, your body will be in darkness. And if your light is darkness, how deep will the darkness be!

PRAYER/MEDITATION

O heavenly Father, grant me the wisdom to live each day as though Christ were coming tomorrow. Show me how to open the hearts and minds of others so that they may feel the love of Christ Jesus that you have shown me. Walk me down a path each day that will place me in the footsteps of our Lord so that I will be ready to meet him when he appears to me tomorrow. For you have lightened my burden and taken away the heavy load that I have carried for so long. You have opened my heart with joy and protected me from the sorrows that have come upon me in the past. So now I can look forward to tomorrow, for I am enriched with the love of Jesus Christ our Lord. Amen.

Reflections

How would you describe your emotional, spiritual, and physical status at this time?

If Christ were coming tomorrow, would you be ready to meet him?

What can you do today to better prepare for tomorrow?

How has Christ lightened your burden in life?

How can you enrich the lives of others?

Values

Lost in a Lifeboat

Mark 4:35–41

That day as evening drew on he said to them, "Let us cross over to the farther shore." Leaving the crowd, they took him away in the boat in which he was sitting, while the other boats accompanied him. It happened that a bad squall blew up. The waves were breaking over the boat and it began to ship water badly. Jesus was in the stern through it all, sound asleep on a cushion. They finally woke him and said to him, "Teacher, does it not matter to you that we are going to drown?" He awoke and rebuked the wind and said to the sea: "Quiet! Be still!" The wind fell off and everything grew calm. Then he said to them, "Why are you so terrified? Why are you lacking in faith?" A great awe overcame them at this. They kept saying to one another, "Who can this be that the wind and the sea obey him?"

PRAYER/MEDITATION

Dear heavenly Father, life here on earth is fragile and short, and yet it can be so beautiful when you are part of it. I am so grateful for all the gifts you have given me. You have pardoned me from my sins and given me the gift of hope. You have given me my past to learn from and the future to spend my knowledge on. You have given me the strength to live and abide in your will. And you have given me your Son, our Lord Jesus Christ, to call upon in times of need. Help me to accept the gifts you have given, and let me not seek more than your plan for me, for in you life is enough. Amen.

Reflections

"I am the light of the world. No follower of mine shall ever walk in darkness; no, he shall possess the light of life" (John 8:12). What does Christ mean by light and darkness? What does this mean to you? How does this message have bearing on your life?

Do you live your life in darkness or do you live your life in the light?

What fears, doubts, or restraints do you have that you cannot give to God? Why not?

What gift that God has given you are you most grateful for?

Complete the Thought

1 Corinthians 12:12–22

The body is one and has many members, but all the members, many though they are, are one body; and so it is with Christ. It was in one Spirit that all of us, whether Jew or Greek, slave or free, were baptized into one body. All of us have been given to drink of the one Spirit. Now the body is not one member, it is many. If the foot should say, "Because I am not a hand I do not belong to the body," would it then no longer belong to the body? If the ear should say, "Because I am not an eye I do not belong to the body," would it then no longer belong to the body? If the body were all eye, what would happen to our hearing? If it were all ear, what would happen to our smelling? As it is, God has set each member of the body in the place he wanted it to be. If all the members were alike, where would the body be? There are, indeed, many different members, but one body. The eye cannot say to the hand, "I do not need you," any more than the head can say to the feet, "I do not need you." Even those members of the body which seem less important are in fact indispensable.

PRAYER/MEDITATION

Lord, when I think about all the world, and that you gave us all creation, I stand in astonishment at the size and complexity of all that it contains. We are all your creatures, we are all different, and yet your knowledge of us all is complete in every detail. You know even our thoughts, our values, and our feelings. Because of your greatness, Lord, I find it difficult to understand you. But I am grateful, Lord, that you have given us your Holy Spirit to live within us and guide us through this complex world you have created. So help me, Holy Spirit, in my unbelief and give me consolation in that which I do not know. Empower me to know you and your will for me, and help me to better understand myself and others in the light of your wisdom. Through Christ our Lord. Amen.

Reflections

"Be compassionate, as your Father is compassionate. Do not judge, and you will not be judged. Do not condemn, and you will not be condemned. Pardon, and you shall be pardoned" (Luke 6:36–37). What do you think Jesus meant by these statements, and how can you better follow them? Do you follow them?

Think about all the knowledge that God has. What can you do to enhance your understanding of God?

Read 1 Corinthians 12:12–31 What part of the body of Christ are you? What are your gifts, how do you use them, and for whom do you use them?

How do you feel about your gifts and your limitations?

The Nuclear War

Romans 14:7–13

None of us lives as his own master and none of us dies as his own master. While we live we are responsible to the Lord, and when we die we die as his servants. Both in life and in death we are the Lord's. That is why Christ died and came to life again, that he might be Lord of both the dead and the living. But you, how can you sit in judgment on your brother? Or you, how can you look down on your brother? We shall all have to appear before the judgment seat of God. It is written, "As surely as I live, says the Lord, every knee shall bend before me and every tongue shall give praise to God."

PRAYER/MEDITATION

O powerful God, sometimes I find myself with so little faith. Yet I criticize others for having less faith than I. I sometimes react to people of a different race and at the same time ridicule others for being prejudicial. I have chosen many of my friends by their manner and appearance, while I preach that we should love and accept all people for who they are. And, Lord, often I look to satisfy my own personal needs while blaming others for not being more charitable. So help me, Lord, to love, cherish, and forgive all of your people, as you have loved and forgiven me. Help me to accept others as one of your creations. And help me to grow in the strength and wisdom of your Son, our Lord, Jesus Christ. Amen.

Reflections

What traits do you like in others?

How do your "good intentions" affect the way you act?

How can you increase your spiritual standing with Christ?

How did Christ show unconditional love for all?

If you knew that someone was saying bad things about you behind your back, how would you treat that person when you were in his presence?

Abigail

John 8:3–11

The scribes and the Pharisees led a woman forward who had been caught in adultery. They made her stand there in front of everyone. "Teacher," they said to him, "this woman has been caught in the act of adultery. In the law, Moses ordered such women to be stoned. What do you have to say about the case?" Jesus bent down and started tracing on the ground with his finger. When they persisted in their questioning, he straightened up and said to them, "Let the man among you who has no sin be the first to cast a stone at her." A second time he bent down and wrote on the ground. Then the audience drifted away one by one, beginning with the elders. This left him alone with the woman, who continued to stand there before him. Jesus finally straightened up and said to her, "Woman, where did they all disappear to? Has no one condemned you?" "No one, sir," she answered. Jesus said, "Nor do I condemn you. You may go. But from now on avoid this sin."

PRAYER/MEDITATION

O Jesus, how very clever and understanding you are when confronting sinners and when faced with people judging others. I can picture those people standing around accusing and condemning her, and you, Lord, stating: "Let the man among you who has no sin be the first to cast a stone at her." And then you begin writing in the sand, and as each sees you writing his sin in the sand, they all turn and walk away. Then you state that you cannot condemn her either, and with respect you caution her to sin no more. O Lord, I pray that you will always remind me of this story when I condemn or accuse others. For you know that I have sinned and have no authority to judge others. Teach me only to love one another, not to judge or condemn them. Bless me with compassion and patience for all my brothers and sisters, and help me to see you in everyone. Amen.

Reflections

Think of the last time you forgave someone else and reflect on the feeling you had.

Have you ever felt not forgiven? How did it make you feel?

Have you noticed that when you do not forgive someone, it is you who must hold on to the uncomfortable feelings of resentment?

Whom do you know who has a "Christ-like" attitude about forgiveness? Why is that person that way? How do you feel in that person's presence?

Perceptive Triads

2 Corinthians 3:9–18

If the ministry of the covenant that condemned had glory, greater by far is the glory of the ministry that justifies. Indeed, when you compare that limited glory with this surpassing glory, the former should be declared no glory at all. If what was destined to pass away was given in glory, greater by far is the glory that endures.

Our hope being such, we act with full confidence. We are not like Moses, who used to hide his face with a veil so that the Israelites could not see the final fading of that glory. Their minds, of course, were dulled. To this very day, when the old covenant is read the veil remains unlifted; it is only in Christ that it is taken away. Even now, when Moses is read a veil covers their understanding. "But whenever he turns to the Lord, the veil will be removed." The Lord is the Spirit, and where the Spirit of the Lord is, there is freedom. All of us, gazing on the Lord's glory with unveiled faces, are being transformed from glory to glory into his very image by the Lord who is the Spirit.

PRAYER/MEDITATION

Holy Spirit, come to me to bless me and dwell in me. You know that I am not all that I pretend to be or all that I want to be or all that I can be. So many times I wear one mask for one occasion and another mask for some other occasion. Help me to rid myself of the masks that blind me to the truth. Spirit of truth and love, help me to become a true spirit of our Lord. Direct my energies toward loving others rather than being preoccupied with trying to impress others. Teach me, Lord, to accept myself with all of my limitations and all of my shortcomings. Help me to accept myself for what I am, as I am, and who I am, and help me to help others to do the same. Show me how to accept myself and others the way you accept us. This I ask through Christ our Lord. Amen.

Reflections

Imagine you are talking to God and he asks you, "Where did I fall short when I made you?" How would you answer?

Suppose you lived in a world where everyone always wore masks and costumes. How would you pick your friends?

What others think of you is important to you. But explain what traits, in yourself and others, are most important and acceptable to you. To others? To God?

You are a teacher in a classroom full of teenagers, and they want to know why they are not accepted by everyone. What do you tell them?

Fun in General

Minimum Level

Mark 7:14–23

He summoned the crowd again and said to them: "Hear me, all of you, and try to understand. Nothing that enters a man from outside can make him impure; that which comes out of him, and only that, constitutes impurity. Let everyone heed what he hears!"

When he got home, away from the crowd, his disciples questioned him about the proverb. "Are you, too, incapable of understanding?" he asked them. "Do you not see that nothing that enters a man from outside can make him impure? It does not penetrate his being, but enters his stomach only and passes into the latrine." Thus did he render all foods clean. He went on: "What emerges from within a man, that and nothing else is what makes him impure. Wicked designs come from the deep recess of the heart: acts of fornication, theft, murder, adulterous conduct, greed, maliciousness, deceit, sensuality, envy, blasphemy, arrogance, an obtuse spirit. All these evils come from within and render a man impure."

PRAYER/MEDITATION

Lord, you have given me so many gifts to be thankful for, but sometimes I feel as though others have been blessed more than I. Help me to understand that we are all blessed with different talents and abilities, and that we should use these talents and abilities to promote love and peace in your kingdom on earth. Give me the sight to look beyond myself to the glory of your reign. And, Lord, help me to understand that it is not by intelligence that we should measure a person. For it is by our acts, deeds, and love for one another that we will all be measured. Grant me the strength and understanding to accept all people exactly the way they are, without judgment, prejudice, and jealousy getting in my way. Amen.

Reflections

Almost everyone has felt uninformed or second-best at one time or another. Think of a time when you felt put down by someone. How did that make you feel?

Is there a subject that you would like to know more about? What can you do to become more informed about that subject?

What are your knowledge boundaries, and what can you do to expand these boundaries?

What are your impurities? How can you take steps to cleanse these impurities from your life?

Think So

Matthew 7:7–12

Ask, and you will receive. Seek, and you will find. Knock, and it will be opened to you. For the one who asks, receives. The one who seeks, finds. The one who knocks, enters. Would one of you hand his son a stone when he asks for a loaf, or a poisonous snake when he asks for a fish? If you, with all your sins, know how to give your children what is good, how much more will your heavenly Father give good things to anyone who asks him! Treat others the way you would have them treat you: this sums up the law and the prophets.

PRAYER/MEDITATION

O precious Lord, sometimes I do not know which way to turn for the answers to all the questions I have now. I feel so lost and alone. I find it hard to turn to others because I am afraid of being misunderstood. Give me the strength, the love and the courage to reach out and be supported by others in the way that I want to be supported. Help them to help me find the answers. And, heavenly Father, give me some direction so that I may find health and happiness in my life. This I ask in the name of your Son, our Lord, Jesus Christ. Amen.

Reflections

If Christ were standing next to you right now, what questions would you have for him?

Whom can you talk to, or where do you turn, to find the answers to difficult questions concerning your personal life?

Think of a time when an important issue came up and you were sure that you had the correct solution, but later your solution did not work out. How did that make you feel? What did you do? How would you handle it today?

What can you do to lessen the frequency of unworkable solutions in your decision making process?

If you were talking to your children, what would you tell them are the important things to know about decision making?